CW01509878

# Starter Sour Made Easy For Beginners

## *How To Make Bread, Pancakes, Buns, Cookies, Pizza Crust And More With Sourdough*

# Introduction

*Have you recently come across the concept of using sourdough starter and instantly got hooked to the idea but don't know what to do to make your very own sourdough starter or even use it to make all manner of chewy and delicious breads, bagels, muffins, crackers, waffles and more?*

*Have you been dreaming of making your own breads, pancakes, cookies, buns, donuts and many more with Sourdough?*

If you've answered YES, keep reading....

**<u>You Are About To Discover How To Leverage The Power Of Sourdough Starter To Make Tasty, Delicious Cakes, Bagels, Cookies, Buns, Donuts, Pancakes, Breads, Crackers, Waffles And More!</u>**

While it has been with us for ages, it's only recently that most people have started to truly appreciate the value of Sourdough. It's not only the foundation of the tastiest breads and other baked goods, but a very potent source of healthy naturally occurring bacteria, vitamins, fiber, minerals and great phytate levels which mean more nutrition, better digestion, healthier blood sugar, healthier gut and a more balanced body system.

Unfortunately, for someone who has never used it before, it can feel difficult and overwhelming to use. It's not uncommon to hear people saying that Sourdough Starters tend to die easily or can get ruined if their handlers aren't super careful, just to say the least.

Is that why you are here?

Have you been asking yourself *how you can handle this amazing product to reap its amazing benefits?*

Perhaps *what it means and how it works as well?*

Have you been wondering *how you can use it to prepare different foods?*

Or maybe *how to get started as someone who's completely new to it?*

If you've been having these or similar concerns or questions, then this cookbook is here for you. From the basics of Sourdough Starter to how you can use it to make nearly anything, this book has everything you need.

**<u>Here's a tiny bit of what you'll learn from it:</u>**

- An overview of Sourdough Starter, including what it is and its special features

- **How to deal with Sourdough discard and take advantage of Sourdough hydration to have the perfect bread texture**

- How to make breads and pancakes using water-based starter and milk-based starter

- **How to use the Sourdough Starter to make rolls, pizzas, discard crackers, bagels, muffins, breads, waffles and many more**

- How to use 100% hydration Sourdough Starter to make cakes, cookies, crepes, breads, buns, donuts, pasta, biscuits and others

**...And so much more!**

It doesn't matter what you've heard about Sourdough Starter before... or the mistakes you've made using it so far.

It doesn't matter how experienced you are in baking or how conversant you are with the science of wheat, yeast and other components of dough.

This simple, beginners' book will make everything seem so easy to you and have you making your first set of healthy Sourdough breads in no time!

Let's begin!

# Table of Contents

# Introduction To Sourdough Starter

A **sourdough starter** is simply a live culture of flour and water. It is how we cultivate the wild yeast in order for it to be useful in baking. So what exactly is wild yeast? Wild yeast is everywhere including in the air, in the flour etc. Hence, when we combine water and flour, it starts to ferment and this activates "wild yeast."

When compared to commercial yeast, wild yeast is a little bit difficult to work with. For starters, as mentioned above, it needs a sour dough starter to be used in baking. It also takes longer to proof, which makes it a bit challenging to work with. However, the results are amazing; its texture and flavor cannot be rivaled.

Let us now look at a few guidelines to follow when preparing your initial sourdough starter:

### *The Kind Of Flour Required*

The choice of flour mainly depends on your preferred outcome in terms of taste, smell and appearance of the final product. Most flours are applicable here such as whole wheat, rye flour, unbleached all purpose flour, spelt flour and Elkhorn wheat flour. In case you want a **gluten-free** alternative, you can substitute regular flour with amaranth flour, quinoa flour, buckwheat flour and brown rice flour.

However, be aware that such flours tend to sour quickly therefore you must feed them up to 3 times per day! It's also important to play around with flour and water ratios when baking as individual flour reacts differently. Furthermore, you should avoid high sugar sweet rice and tapioca flours due to their high tendency to grow molds.

### *Containers To Store Your Sourdough Starter*

You need a container that is at least twice the size of your sourdough starter to give it sufficient room to grow and expand. The sourdough starter should also have enough access to air. In addition, you may need to crack lids open as soon as the sourdough starter begins to double in size to avoid possible **explosion**. You can use containers such as:

- Glass mason jars

- A lockable food storage container

- Stoneware crock

Whichever the container you use, keep it clean. You'll notice some crusty bits of dried flour at the top of the container so you'll need to remove the sourdough starter and clean it up.

### How Often To Feed Sourdough Starter

It depends on where you make your sourdough starter in. If you leave the starter on the counter, and loosely covered, try feeding it at 12 to 24 hours intervals based on room temperature. If your room is hot, it requires more feedings and if cold the less often you can feed it. Check for signs such as reduction in size, doubling in size or accumulation of some liquid on top, which signals for more feeding.

In case you may put your sourdough starter in the fridge, particularly if you bake less often then you need to feed it at least 1 per week. You'll need to bring the chilled sourdough starter to room temperature before using it. Then you should cleanup any dried-up content after feeding.

### After How Long Is Starter Ready To Use?

Generally, the sourdough starter is ready for use once it has doubled in size and looks bubbly, i.e. has ultimately filled most air holes. Alternatively, do a **float test** by scooping 1 teaspoon of the starter and dropping it in a glass of water. In case the sourdough starter floats, it's ready for use! However, if it sinks, you'll need to feed it once more or just allow more time for it to be **active**.

## Sourdough Discard

The "discard" is the clear liquid on top of the sourdough starter that you pour off when feeding to allow more room for yeast and bacteria growth. It advisable to maintain a starter to water to flour ratio of 1:1:1 that you must discard part of the starter to control final yield. In addition, a reduced volume of the sourdough starter means that less yeast cells are fighting to get enough flour "to eat".

There are 3 different ways of dealing with the discard:

- Throw it away anywhere far from your drain as it often becomes cement-like after drying

- Feed the discard for a few days until it becomes active again to be used for baking

- Use it as is to make unfed sourdough discard starter bread recipes!

## Sourdough Hydration

The hydration level in baking refers to the amount of liquid or water in the dough; the more water the dough has, the higher the hydration percentage and vice versa. The hydration levels play a big part in sourdough baking since it controls the final texture of your bread. Furthermore, it determines how the dough will react during the mixing, fermenting process and shaping the dough. Since fermentation of sough-dough bread may result in a tighter crumb, it is advisable to use **wetter dough**.

For sourdough starter, keep the hydration level to around 100 percent, which means the amount of water you use should be **equal** to the amount of flour. However, you might prefer to keep your starter at either lower or higher concentrations for various reasons.

For instance you may need a **thicker or stiffer** sourdough starter so you'll add less amount of water for a lower hydration level. You may also need wetter **dough** at around 125 percent hydration level to make the starter easier to mix.

Here is a comparison of various hydration levels for sourdough starters:

## 1. *Stiff Starter*

- Usually has a 50 – 70% hydration level

- Fed less often that is it can go for more hours without feedings

- It's harder to mix due to the thick consistency

- It yields a more sour flavor in the sour dough bread due to increased production of **acetic acid**

## 2. *Wet Starter*

- Usually120 – 130% in hydration levels

- It requires that you feed it more often since it absorbs flour fast

- Easier to mix due to the wet consistency

- It yields a milder flavor as it favors growth of **lactic acid**

NOTE*:*

Whether choosing a 100% Hydration level or otherwise, you should always feed your sourdough starter by weight and not by volume. This helps avoid possible fluctuations in mixing ratios that may negatively affect hydration levels. For instance add 100g of water to 100 grams of flour to simplify your mixing and feeding.

With that information, it's time to make your first sourdough starter from scratch!

# Sourdough Starter Recipe 1

This recipe comes in three variations, depending on ingredients used.

## Variation 1: Water-Based Starter

### Ingredients

1 cup all-purpose flour or whole wheat flour

½ cup water

### *Equipment*

Baker's scale

Offset spatula

1-quart container with lid

### Directions

1. First, mix and stir together 1/2 cup of cool water with a cup of flour in a 1-quart mason jar or any other glass container to help track your sourdough starter growth.

2. Loosely cover the container for approximately 24 hours and set it on the counter at about 70°F or just at a warm temperature.

3. In day 2, discard approximately 1/2 cup of the starter or just half of the starter and then add in 1 cup of fresh flour along with fresh 1/2 cup of water.

4. Mix the ingredients, and stir well until incorporated. Let the mixture sit for another 24 hours or so.

5. In day 3, you'll be required to feed the starter twice. In the morning, discard most of the starter and reserve just 1/2 cup.

6. Feed it again with 1/2 cup of fresh water and another 1 cup of flour. Mix well and let the starter rest for approximately 12 hours. Then repeat the discarding process and feed it again the evening.

7. In day 4, repeat the procedure in day 3, discard while leaving 1/2 cup of the starter and feed it twice.

8. In 5 day, repeat the directions of day 3 only this time discard and feed the starter just once. Let it rest for 14 hours.

9. Depending on how your starter is progressing, at day 6 you might notice many bubbles to an extent that it has almost

doubled in size. This means that the sourdough starter is almost ready so just give it one 1 more feeding.

10. In case you don't note significant changes, discard and reserve 1/2 cup of starter. Then feed it twice at 12 hours intervals.

11. At day 7 or so, the starter should be ready. Here it should double in size within 6 to 8 hours after last feeding.

## Sourdough Starter With Packaged Yeast

As mentioned earlier, starter refers to homemade fermented yeast. Usually, getting good yeast just from the environment as mentioned can be challenging and tricky; thus, you can get some help from store-bought use in order to kick-start the whole process.

You have the option of making yeast-based sourdough starter with either water or milk. A water based starter recipe is useful for making pancakes, biscuits, dinner rolls and crusty bread. A milk based sourdough starter is most suitable for quick breads, coffee cakes and other baked bread desserts that require sugar flavor.

# Variation 2: Water-Based Yeast Sourdough

## Ingredients

1 cup warm water

3 cups all-purpose flour

1 package dry yeast, mixed with ¼ cup warm water

2 tablespoons sugar

2 large mealy potatoes, peeled and halved

## Directions

1. Put the potatoes in a big saucepan with enough water to cover the potatoes fully.

2. Gently boil the potatoes until they fall apart. Do not drain the potatoes but instead pass them through a sieve and allow them to cool down.

3. Now add in water to make up 3 cups of the mixture. Pour the mixture in a large ceramic or glass container or bowl.

4. Stir in 2 cups of flour, dissolved yeast and sugar using a nonmetal spoon. Mix the ingredients until you obtain a creamy and smooth mixture.

5. Cover the mixture with a kitchen towel and place it in a warm setting, 70 degrees F.

6. Let the mixture stand for approximately 24 hours or until the batter develops a pleasant sour smell.

7. Stir in a cup of warm water along with the rest of the flour. Cover using a towel and allow the mixture to stand for about 2 to 3 days.

8. Transfer the sourdough starter to a tightly covered plastic or glass container and keep it refrigerated.

9. To use your sourdough starter, just stir the liquid on the surface and get the amount that you need. Let the chilled starter come to room temperature.

10. Replace the volume you have removed by adding in equal parts of water and flour. For instance add 1/2 cup each of flour and water to replenish 1 cup of starter.

# Variation 3: Milk-Based Sourdough

This starter is sweeter and has lactic acid produced from fermentation of milk and sugar. The lactic acid helps weaken gluten in wheat and this yields tender crumb texture!

## Ingredients

1 package dry yeast, mixed with ¼ cup warm water

1 cup sugar

2 cups all-purpose flour

2 cups milk

## Directions

1. Mix together 1 cup of flour and milk along with the dissolved yeast and the sugar in a ceramic or glass bowl.

2. Mix the mixture using a nonmetal spoon until you have a smooth and creamy consistency.

3. Stir in the rest of the flour and milk, 1 cup each. Cover the ingredients using a clean towel and place in a warm place, approximately 70 degrees F.

4. Let the sourdough starter stand for about 24 hours, or until it develops a pleasant but sour taste.

5. Transfer the mixture to a plastic or glass container, close it tight and keep it chilled.

6. Keep stirring the contents on a day to day basis for around 5 days. After the five days, you can remove from the fridge and let it come to room temperature before using.

7. To use, scoop the amount that you require, and then replenish with equal parts of milk and flour and a half part of sugar.

8. If using 1 cup of sourdough starter, add in 1/4 cup sugar along with 1/2 cup each of milk and flour.

## How to Use the Sourdough Starter

### Crusty Bread

### Yields 4 small loaves

### Ingredients

4 to 5 cups bread flour,

1 teaspoon salt

2 cups water-based sourdough

1 package dry yeast

1 tablespoon sugar

1 cup warm water

### Directions

1. First mix water, yeast and sugar in a large mixing bowl and stir until the yeast is full dissolved.

2. Add in 2 cups of flour, salt and sourdough. Beat the mixture thoroughly until the dough has pulled away from the sides of the container.

3. Now measure about 1 cup of flour and sprinkle some of the flour over the work area. Turn out the dough.

4. Knead the dough as you sprinkle on the flour until there is full absorption of the 1 cup of flour.

5. Knead some more dough until you obtain smooth and non-sticky dough. Your dough should easily spring back in case you poke it with a finger.

6. Put the flour in a greased bowl and cover it using a plastic wrap. Put it in a cool place and let it rest until doubled in size.

7. At this point turn the dough on the well floured work surface and knead it another time until it's smooth and glossy.

8. Transfer the dough back to the greased container and cover it with some plastic wrap.

9. Put the dough in a cool place and let it rise a second time until doubled. Meanwhile grease 2 small pans or bigger baguette pans and sprinkle with some cornmeal.

10. Turn the dough on the well-floured surface and shape it into 2 big loaves.

11. Lightly dust the long loaves with sifted flour and move it to the prepared pans. Cover the bread dough with plastic wrap.

12. Allow the dough to rise until doubled and then create 3 diagonal slashes down the two breads.

13. Dust it another time with the sifted flour and then bake in a preheated oven at 450 degrees F until nicely browned, or for 25 to 35 minutes.

**Walnut Bread**

**Yields 1 loaf**

**Ingredients**

½ cup walnuts, coarsely chopped

1 cup milk-based sourdough

1 cup applesauce

¼ cup vegetable oil

1 large egg

¼ teaspoon allspice

½ teaspoon cinnamon

¾ teaspoon salt

½ teaspoon baking soda

2 teaspoons baking powder

½ cup light brown sugar

1 ¾ cups all-purpose flour, scoop measured

**Directions**

1. Preheat your oven to 350 degrees F. Meanwhile grease a 9 by 15 loaf pan.

2. Sift the flour, baking powder, baking soda, sugar and salt in the bowl of your electric mixer.

3. Add in the allspice and cinnamon, and have the mixer on low briefly to incorporate the dry ingredients.

4. W together vegetable oil and eggs in a different bowl and then pour in the applesauce. Mix well to blend.

5. Slowly add in the egg and oil mixture into the dry ingredients, with the mixer setting at low speed.

6. Add in the sourdough starter and beat the mixture until well blended. Add in the walnuts and stir well.

7. At this point pour the contents in a well greased pan and bake for approximately 50 to 60 minutes. You can cover the contents for the last 10 minutes to prevent over-browning.

8. To check if the loaf is cooked through, just insert a wooden stick and check if it comes out clean.

9. Put the pan on a cooling rack for about 10 minutes, then turn out the bread and let it cool fully until you're ready to serve.

10. You can serve the walnut bread as an after-school snack if you like.

## Pancakes

## Yields 12 large pancakes

## Ingredients

1 cup water-based sourdough

3 tablespoons butter, melted

2 large eggs

1½ cups milk

¾ teaspoon salt

½ teaspoon baking soda

2 teaspoons baking powder

1 tablespoon sugar

1 ½ cups all-purpose flour

## Directions

1. Mix together baking soda, baking powder, sugar, flour and salt in a large mixing bowl. Whisk the ingredients until well incorporated.

2. Whisk together butter, eggs, and milk in a different bowl and make a well in the dry ingredients. Add in the sourdough starter.

3. Add in the whisked egg mixture and stir using a wooden spoon until moistened. Your batter should be having a few lumps.

4. Put the griddle over medium high heat and add in some oil.

5. As soon as the griddle is hot, stir the batter and add a little more milk if you need to achieve a heavy cream consistency.

6. Ladle about 1/4 cupfuls of the batter onto your griddle and cook until the bubbles around the outside of the pancakes are broken.

7. Flip over the pancakes and cook the second side until cooked through.

8. Repeat with the rest of the batter. You can add more milk if need be so as to maintain a nice consistency. Keep the pancakes hot or warm until you're ready to serve. You can top with warm maple syrup if you like.

## Streusel Coffee Cake

### Yields a 9"x13" cake

### Ingredients

½ teaspoon baking soda

2 teaspoons baking powder

1/2 cup vegetable oil

½ teaspoon salt

2 large eggs

1 cup granulated sugar

¾ cup milk

2 cups milk-based sourdough

2 ½ teaspoons cinnamon

2 tablespoons butter

½ cup light brown sugar

2 ¼ cups all-purpose flour, scoop measured

**Directions**

1. Preheat your oven to 350 degrees F. Meanwhile grease a 9 by 13 baking pan.

2. Mix together 1/4 cup of flour, 1 teaspoon of cinnamon, butter and brown sugar in a small bowl.

3. Cut the mixture in using a knife until its crumbly, and then set aside.

4. Beat the milk, sourdough starter, and sugar in the bowl of an electric mixer. Beat in some vegetable oil and the eggs.

5. Mix together the 2 cups of flour, salt, baking soda, baking powder and the reserved 1 teaspoon of cinnamon. Whisk the ingredients until well blended.

6. Slowly mix in the dry ingredients, with the mixer set at low speed. Then pour the mixture into a well prepared pan.

7. Bake until if you insert a wooden pick at the center, it comes out clean, or for 30 to 40 minutes.

8. Put the coffee cake in a rack to cool down. You can top with cinnamon flavored crumb topping.

# Sourdough Starter Recipe 2

## Equipment

Baker's Scale

Offset Spatula

Wide Mouth Mason jar with Lid

## *Ingredients*

1/3 cup whole-wheat flour

5 cups unbleached all-purpose flour

Water

## Directions

1. Begin by adding 50 grams of all-purpose flour and 50 grams of whole-wheat flour into a clean glass jar.

2. Add in 100 grams of water and stir thoroughly with a spatula until the mixture is smooth with no clumps.

3. Using a wet napkin, clean the inside of the jar well and cover it loosely with a lid or a fabric. Allow the setup to rest at room temperature for a full day.

4. In the second day, stir the mixture, and then clean the inside of the rim of your jar. Cover the jar and allow it to rest for another 24 hours.

5. Between days 3 all the way to day 7, keep adding 50 grams of the sourdough starter to a clean glass jar and discard the rest. Then add 100 grams of water and 100 grams of all-purpose flour and then stir the mixture thoroughly. Clean the inside of the glass jar well and then put a rubber band to mark the sourdough starter level.

6. Cover the contents loosely and allow to rest for an entire 24 hours. Your starter can be used once it rises and falls for a number of consecutive days.

7. Feed the sourdough starter up to 7 days of doubling to make it stronger. You can do a **float test** to check if it's ready for use.

8. Store the ready sourdough starter in a fridge, while loosely covered until ready to bake. Save any discarded starter in the fridge in a different glass jar for separate discard recipes.

9. In case you live in a warm, humid or high altitude area, feed 50 grams of all-purpose flour and another 50 grams of whole wheat starting on day 3.

10. Do a second feeding about 12 hours from the first 2 teaspoons of water and 2 tablespoons of flour until the sourdough starter is ready to use.

# How To Use The Sourdough Starter

## Cinnamon Rolls

**Servings: 12**

### Equipment

Pastry Brush

Cheese Grater

Bench-Scraper

Mixing Bowls

12" Cast Iron Skillet

### *Ingredients*

1/2 teaspoon baking soda

1 teaspoon baking powder

3/4 teaspoon fine sea salt

2 tablespoons granulated sugar or honey

1 cup buttermilk or other milk

1/2 cup sourdough starter stirred down discard

2 1/2 cups all-purpose flour

8 tablespoons cold butter

*Cinnamon-Sugar Filling*

4 tablespoons melted butter

2 teaspoons ground cinnamon

3/4 cup light brown sugar

*Cinnamon Roll Glaze*

2 tablespoons milk

1 teaspoon vanilla extract

1 tablespoon melted butter

1 cup powdered sugar

## Directions

1. Make the dough approximately 12 hours before baking. Grate the cold butter using a cheese grater and transfer the butter into a mixing bowl.

2. Add in the flour into the butter and mix. Stir in the sourdough starter discard, honey and buttermilk.

3. Use a spatula to mix until well incorporated. Cover the bowl and allow it to rest on the counter for about 12 hours or so. Do not add any baking powder, baking soda or salt at this step.

4. Meanwhile heat your oven to 375 degrees F and then butter a 12-inch iron skillet and set aside. In a small bowl, mix together cinnamon and sugar and set aside. Combine the ingredients for making the glaze in another bowl and set aside too.

5. At this point, mix baking soda, salt and baking powder using a fork in a small bowl until there are no visible clumps. Using your hands, sprinkle the baking soda and salt mixture on the dough.

6. Flour your work surface and put the dough on the work surface. Flour the top of your dough and roll the dough using a rolling pin into 12 by 22 inch rectangle.

7. Get a pastry brush and coat the top surface of the dough with some melted butter. Evenly sprinkle the sugar and cinnamon mixture onto the dough leaving a 1/2 inch space along the edges.

8. Roll the dough into a log shape, beginning at one side. Cut the dough log into 12 equal sized pieces using a bench scrapper.

9. Put the pieces into a cast iron skillet, a spring-form pan, a baking dish or a baking pan. Leave some space between individual dough pieces to allow for expansion.

10. Finally bake cinnamon rolls until the tops are golden brown, or for 30 to 40 minutes. Remove the rolls from the oven and glaze while still hot.

11. In case you find the dough sticky and impossible to roll, lower the amount of milk by 50 grams in the original mix. You can then add the milk gradually until you achieve the preferred hydration level. Also replace honey with granulated sugar.

12. To make your roll glaze lighter, just add a teaspoon of milk along with a cup of powdered sugar. Stir and add a little more milk until you get your preferred consistency.

13. You can also use active sourdough starter. Just add salt into the original mix, then cut the cinnamon rolls out and allow them rise for approximately 1 to 1 1/2 hours and then bake.

## Sourdough Pizza Crust

### Yields: 4 crusts

### Equipment

12" Cast Iron Skillet

Kitchen Scale

Mixing Bowls

### *Ingredients*

*Sourdough pizza crust*

1.5 cups water

3.5 cups + 1 tablespoon all-purpose flour

1/3 cup + 2 teaspoons whole wheat flour

2 tablespoons olive oil

2 teaspoons fine sea salt

1/2 cup sourdough starter discard

*Pizza toppings*

Pizza sauce

Other preferred toppings

**Directions**

1. The night before baking, mix the ingredients for making the pizza crust in a mixing bowl and mix using your hands until well blended together.

2. Keep the bowl covered and let the dough ferment at room temperature preferably overnight.

3. The following morning do a set of folds and stretches. Just wet your hands and pull one side of the dough over itself, while still in the bowl. Turn the bowl and repeat this procedure on all sides of your dough until you do a full circle.

4. Keep the bowl covered in the fridge for approximately 36 hours then you can proceed with the cooking.

5. On that night, remove the dough from the refrigerator and put it on your counter for about 30 minutes to come to room temperature.

6. Cut the dough into 4 equal portions and place them on a well floured surface. Shape each of the pieces into a ball, and then cover the dough balls with a tea towel for approximately 30 minutes.

7. Set your oven to broiler's setting and then over medium-high heat setting, heat up a cast iron skillet. Meanwhile, press the dough on a floured surface with your hands to form an 8 inch circle. You can add more flour to prevent any sticking.

8. As soon as the cast iron skillet is very hot, arrange the dough circles onto the skillet and cover with the sauce and your preferred toppings. Cook the contents until the bottom of the crust begins to turn brown and charred, or for 5 to 6 minutes.

9. Transfer the cast iron skillet to the broiler and bake the top of your pizza crust for another 4 to 5 minutes. Then remove from the broiler, slice and enjoy hot!

10. In case you found the dough hard to shape or very sticky, reduce the amount of water by 50 grams then add the water gradually to achieved desired hydration level. You can also swap 400 grams of all purpose flour with 100 grams of whole wheat flour as whole wheat absorbs more water.

11. In case you don't have a cast iron skillet, cook the pizza on a nonstick skillet on a stove-top then slide onto a baking sheet once ready to go under a broiler. If the dough seems harder to shape into a pizza crust, allow it to rest for about 15 minutes.

12. To freeze the dough, make it into balls, put each ball into separate resealable freezer bag, and keep frozen for not more than 3 months. Then you can thaw in the fridge for another 12 hours then bring to room temperature.

## Sourdough Bagels

**Servings: 8**

**Ingredients**

1 tablespoon granulated sugar

4 cups + 2 tablespoons bread flour or all-purpose flour

2 teaspoons fine sea salt

2 tablespoons honey or sugar

1 cup plus 1 tablespoon water

1/2 cup sourdough active starter

*Optional Toppings*

Shredded cheese

Poppy seeds

Salt

Everything Bagel Seasoning

Sesame seeds

**Directions**

# Starter Sourdough

1. Begin by making an active sourdough starter. Just add 2 grams of starter, 50 grams of flour and 50 grams of water.

2. Allow the mixture to rise until it has doubled or for about 4 to 12 hours depending on how warm the surrounding is. Then you can mix with the bagel dough.

3. Now stir together honey, water, salt and the active starter using a spatula. Add the bread flour and blend the ingredients together using your hands.

4. Transfer the stiff dough to the mixer and process on lowest speed for approximately to 7 minutes. You can also knead by hand for about 10 minutes.

5. Then cover the container and allow the dough to rest at room temperature for about 8 to 12 hours.

6. Get a parchment paper and line your baking sheet. Then turn the dough on a well-floured surface and cut the dough into 8 equal portions.

7. Shape each individual portion into a ball and then put the ball on your work surface. Poke a hole straight down the center of the dough using your thumb to make a bagel.

8. Pick the bagel, reshape it into a ring and place into on the parchment paper lined baking sheet.

9. Repeat the procedure with the other 7 balls and cover the balls with a clean towel. Allow to rise until puffy, or for 30 seconds.

10. Preheat your oven to 425 degrees F. Then add 3 inches of water high in a large pot and bring to a boil. Add a tablespoon of sugar.

11. As soon as the bagels have risen, add the dough to the hot water and boil about 3 to 4 pieces of dough on both sides for approximately 2 minutes. Take care not to overcrowd the pot.

12. Remove the bagels from the hot water using a mesh strainer and let them rest on the parchment paper until cooled down. Then dip the bagel into your preferred toppings and return to the parchment paper.

13. Bake the bagels at 425 degrees F until golden brown, or for 25 to 28 minutes.

14. Store the bagels covered for not more than 7 days. You can also cool them fully then freeze them while wrapped in plastic wrap for not more than 3 months. To reheat just thaw on the counter, cut in half and heat in the toaster.

15. In case you live in warmer or high humidity area, reduce the amount of water by 50 grams then gradually add water until you achieve the best consistency.

## Sourdough Discard Crackers

### Servings: 4

### Ingredients

2 tablespoons melted butter

3/4 cup stirred down discarded sourdough starter

2 teaspoons dried Herbs de Provence herbs

1/4 teaspoon salt

1/4 teaspoon fine sea salt

*Optional*

Grated hard cheeses

Fresh herbs

### Directions

1. Preheat your oven to 325 degrees F. Meanwhile get a parchment paper and line your baking sheet. Then in a mixing bowl, melt the butter and allow to cool.

2. Measure out the sourdough starter, salt and the dried herbs into the bowl that has melted butter. Mix well until blended.

3. Using a spatula evenly spread the mixture onto the parchment paper in a thin layer. Season with some salt on top.

4. Bake the crackers for approximately 10 minutes. Then remove them from the oven and score them.

5. Bake the crackers until the crackers are golden brown or for another 40 to 50 minutes. Check them after about 40 minutes to ensure they don't over-bake.

6. Allow them to cool fully and then break into squares. You can store the crackers in an airtight container for no more than 7 days.

7. You can add grated hard cheeses and fresh herbs to add flavor. Then you don't have to score the crackers as the baked cracker sheet will break down after cooling down.

# Banana Nut Muffins

## Servings: 12 slices

## Ingredients

*Wet Ingredients*

1/2 cup sourdough starter aged discard

1 teaspoon vanilla extract

3 tablespoons sour cream

3 very ripe bananas (about 1 cup, mashed)

2 large eggs

1 cup sugar

8 tablespoons melted unsalted butter

*Dry Ingredients*

1 cup chopped walnuts

1 teaspoon fine sea salt

1/2 teaspoon baking soda

2 teaspoons baking powder

2 cups all-purpose flour

**Equipment**

Spatula

Measuring cups/spoons

Mixing Bowls

Muffin tin

## Directions

1. Preheat your oven to 350 degrees F. Meanwhile lightly grease or instead line 12 cup muffin tin with parchment paper liners.

2. Whisk together baking soda, baking powder and flour in a bowl and set the mixture aside.

3. Using a fork, mash the bananas in a different bowl until smooth. In a mixing bowl, melt the butter and then add in the sugar.

4. Mix the sugar and butter. Now add in sourdough starter discard, sour cream, mashed banana, eggs and vanilla extract. Mix until well incorporated.

5. Mix in the dry ingredients into the wet ingredients using a spatula until well blended. Then slowly fold in 2/3 cups of walnuts.

6. Transfer the batter into the muffin tin and top with the reserved 1/3 cup of walnuts. Bake until if you insert a toothpick in the center it comes out clean, or for 20 to 25 minutes.

7. Transfer the muffins to a cooling rack. You can store the muffins up to 4 days in an airtight container, or alternatively freeze individual muffins wrapped in foil then place in a freezer bag.

*Note:*

You need to use an "aged" sourdough starter, so you should let your starter sit in the fridge for at least 1 week before baking with it. This allows the acid to buildup so as to produce a sour flavor.

## Sourdough English Muffins

**Servings: 10**

**Ingredients**

1/4 cup cornmeal

1 teaspoon fine sea salt

3 cups all-purpose flour

1 cup milk

1 tablespoon honey

1/2 cup active sourdough starter "levain"

### *Equipment*

Non-stick skillet with cover

Tea towel

Parchment Paper

Baking Sheet

Stand Mixer (optional)

Mixing Bowl

# Starter Sourdough

## Directions

1. Make an active starter by mixing 25 grams of sourdough starter discard and 50 grams each flour and water. Allow the flour to rise until doubled or for 4 to 12 hours.

2. The night before, add all the ingredients apart from the corn meal to a big bowl and mix thoroughly using your hands.

3. Cover and allow the dough to rest for approximately 30 to 60 minutes, and then turn the dough into a well floured surface. Knead the dough for around 5 minutes. You can also knead using a stand mixer with a hook attachment at low speed setting for 5 minutes.

4. Put the dough in a bowl, tightly cover with lid and allow to ferment at 65 to 70 degrees F for about 10 to 14 hours.

5. The following morning, transfer the dough onto a well-floured work surface and flour the top of the dough. Use your fingertips to press it until it gets to 0.5 inch of thickness.

6. Get a 3 inch biscuit cutter and cut a number of rounds and put them on a baking sheet sprinkled with some cornmeal.

7. Top the dough with the reserved cornmeal and cover the contents with a clean tea towel. Let the dough rise for about 1 hour.

8. Heat a non stick, skillet at low heat settings and then put the 4 muffins spaced 2 inches apart in the hot skillet.

9. Cover and cook one side of the muffins for 4 minutes over very low heat and then turn them and cook for another 4 minutes. Check if the center of the muffin reaches 200 degrees F for doneness.

10. In case you live in a humid or warm place, just reduce the amount of milk by approximately 30 grams then swap honey with granulated sugar to reduce stickiness. You can add in more water if you find the dough stiff.

11. You can keep the muffins in the freezer for not more than 3 months.

## Sourdough Coffee Cake

**Servings: 9**

**Ingredients**

*Crumble Topping*

2 teaspoons ground cinnamon

1/2 cup all-purpose flour

1/2 cup light brown sugar

4 tablespoons melted butter

1 cup chopped pecans (optional)

*Cinnamon Sugar Filling*

2 teaspoons ground cinnamon

1/3 cup all-purpose flour

1/3 cup light brown sugar

*Coffee Cake Batter*

2 cups all-purpose flour

2 teaspoons baking powder

1 teaspoon fine sea salt

1 cup buttermilk

1/2 cup sourdough starter discard

1/2 cup sour cream

2 teaspoons vanilla extract

2 large eggs

1/2 cup granulated sugar

1/2 cup light brown sugar

8 tablespoons softened butter

## Directions

1. To prepare the crumble topping, just melt some butter in a bowl and then stir in cinnamon and light brown sugar until smooth.

2. Add in pecans and the flour and then stir again until the mixture forms a clumpy mass. Set it aside and allow it to cool.

3. Meanwhile make the cinnamon sugar filling. Just stir the light brown sugar, flour and the cinnamon in a small bowl and set the mixture aside.

4. To prepare the cake batter, begin by preheating your oven to 350 degrees F and then coat an 8 by 8 inch baking sheet with cooking spray or butter.

5. Mix the butter, granulated sugar and the light brown sugar in a mixing bowl until smooth.

6. Add in milk, sourdough starter, sour cream, vanilla extract, eggs, baking powder and salt to the bowl. Stir the mixture until incorporated. Add in the flour and blend well.

7. Add half the batter into the prepared baking dish and sprinkle with the sugar and cinnamon mixture evenly across the batter.

8. Slowly pour the rest of the batter over the sugar and cinnamon mixture and cover. Carefully spread the batter evenly using a spatula. Breakup the crumble topping using your fingers and sprinkle it over the contents.

9. Bake the coffee cake until when you insert a toothpick in the middle it comes out clean, or for approximately 40 to 45 minutes.

10. You can store any leftovers in a container for not more than two days, or instead store in the fridge for a maximum of 7 days.

11. To freeze the coffee cake, let it cool fully and then wrap each cake square with plastic wrap. Put the wrapped cake in a freezer friendly container for not more than 3 months.

12. To reheat the frozen cake, let it thaw first by warming it in the microwave for 1-second intervals. You can also put on a baking sheet lined with parchment paper and then warm in the oven set at 350 degrees until heated through, or for around 10 minutes.

## Sourdough Banana Bread

### Servings: 12 slices

### Ingredients

*Wet Ingredients*

1/2 cup sourdough starter discard

1 teaspoon vanilla extract

3 tablespoons sour cream

3 medium very ripe mashed bananas

2 large eggs

1 cup sugar

8 tablespoons unsalted butter

*Dry Ingredients*

1 teaspoon fine sea salt

1/2 teaspoon baking soda

2 teaspoons baking powder

2 cups all-purpose flour

## Equipment

Spatula

Measuring cups/spoons

Mixing Bowls

9" x 5" loaf pan

## Directions

1. Preheat your oven to 350 degrees F. Meanwhile, lightly coat a 9 by 5 inch loaf pan with grease or oil.

2. Whisk the all-purpose flour, baking powder and salt in a boil until incorporated and then set the mixture aside. Using a fork, mash the bananas in another bowl and set aside.

3. Add butter in a heat-safe bowl and melt it in the microwave. Add in the sugar and mix using a spatula until well blended.

4. Add in the sourdough starter discard, mashed banana, vanilla extract and the sour cream and stir the contents to incorporate.

5. Pour the wet mixture into the dry mixture and stir until blended together. If you like, you can fold in 1/2 cup of chopped walnuts using a spatula and mix well.

6. Add the batter into the loaf pan and bake until if you insert a toothpick into the bread it comes out clean, or for approximately 50 to 60 minutes.

7. Let the banana bread cool down in the loaf pan for about 15 minutes then transfer to a cooling rack until fully cooled down.

8. You can store the banana bread for a maximum of 3 days in a container with a lid or when wrapped in plastic.

9. Alternatively store the bread frozen sealed in a plastic wrap or foil for not more than 3 months.

## Sourdough Pumpkin Bread

## Servings: 12 slices

## Ingredients

*Wet Ingredients*

1 15oz. can pumpkin puree

1 teaspoon vanilla extract

1/4 cup fresh orange juice

1/2 cup sourdough starter discard

1 large egg

1.5 cups light brown sugar

8 tablespoons unsalted butter

*Dry Ingredients*

1/2 teaspoon baking soda

2 teaspoons baking powder

1 teaspoon fine sea salt

2.5 teaspoons pumpkin pie spice

# Starter Sourdough

2 cups all-purpose flour

## Equipment

9" x 5" bread loaf pan

## Directions

1. Preheat your oven to 350 degrees F and oil lightly a 9 by 5 inch loaf pan with oil or butter.

2. Mix all-purpose flour, pumpkin pie spice, baking soda, baking powder and salt in a large bowl and set aside.

3. Melt the butter in a bowl and add in light brown sugar. Cream the mixture together using a spatula until well incorporated.

4. Add in the sourdough starter discard, orange juice, vanilla extract, egg and the pumpkin puree. Combine the ingredients well.

5. Add in the wet mixture into the bowl with the dry ingredients and stir well until the mixture has blended well.

6. At this point add the batter into the prepared loaf pan and bake until cooked through, or for approximately 55 to 60 minutes. Use a toothpick to test for done-ness.

7. Let the pumpkin bread cool for around 15 minutes and then transfer it to a wire rack to cool down.

8. You can store the bread for 3 to 4 days while lightly covered in a container or instead keep it frozen for about 3 months wrapped in a plastic bag.

# Sourdough French Toast

## Servings: 6

## Ingredients

2 tablespoons butter

2 tablespoons vegetable oil

6 slices sourdough bread (3/4" thick)

*Custard ingredients*

1 teaspoon vanilla extract

2 tablespoons white sugar

1/4 teaspoon ground nutmeg

1/2 teaspoon ground cinnamon

1/4 teaspoon fine sea salt

1 cup heavy cream

3 large eggs

## Directions

1. Preheat your oven to 400 degrees F and then put a baking sheet in the oven.

2. Heat a skillet over low to medium heat with some butter and oil. In a bowl add in nutmeg, cinnamon, vanilla extract, sugar, heavy cream, eggs and salt. This custard mixture should cook slowly without burning.

3. Add the mixture into a shallow baking dish and soak in 2 slices of bread each about 3/4 inches thick for approximately 10 minutes on each side.

4. Cook the slices for about 3 to 4 minutes on each side. Meanwhile add in the next 2 slices in the custard mixture.

5. Transfer the coated slices onto the baking sheet in the oven and keep them hot until you're ready to eat them.

6. You can use a mixture of vegetable oil and butter to prevent possible butter burning.

# Sourdough Pancakes Or Waffles

## Servings: 12 pancakes or 4 standard-sized waffles

## Ingredients

*Overnight Batter Ingredients*

2 cups all-purpose flour

4 tablespoons melted butter

1 teaspoon vanilla extract

3 tablespoons white sugar or honey

2 large lightly beaten eggs

1 cup buttermilk or milk

3/4 cup sourdough starter stirred down discard

*Additional ingredients*

1 teaspoon fine sea salt

1 teaspoon baking powder

1 teaspoon baking soda

Starter Sourdough

## *Equipment*

Waffle Iron

Griddle

Whisk

Mixing Bowl

## **Directions**

1. Whisk together all-purpose flour, vanilla extract, honey, eggs, melted butter and the sourdough starter in a large mixing bowl.

2. Cover the bowl and allow the mixture to rest at room temperature for up to 12 hours, or preferably overnight.

3. The following day add in baking soda, salt and baking powder to the batter and stir well. Cover the contents and allow the batter to rest as you preheat a waffle iron or a griddle.

4. To make the pancakes, let the griddle get very hot, then thinly grease it. Add in 1/4 of the batter and shape it into a circle.

5. Cook the pancake for approximately 3 minutes or until the bottom is golden and the bubbles cover the top of the pancake. Flip and cook the other side for another 3 minutes or until golden brown.

6. To make waffles, heat the waffle iron and then grease it lightly with cooking oil.

7. Add in 3/4 cups of the batter to the center of the waffle iron, and then slowly spread the batter.

8. Cook for approximately 3 to 6 minutes or until the waffle is golden brown.

9. In case you want to make the batter that morning, combine all ingredients in a mixing bowl and then cover with a kitchen towel. Let it rest for approximately 30 minutes and then cook.

10. You can keep the batter refrigerated for a maximum of 2 days.

11. Store the waffles or pancakes in a sealable container in the fridge for up to 7 days or in a freezer for not more than 3 months.

12. To serve frozen waffles or pancakes just reheat in the oven for 10 to 15 minutes at 375 degrees F or in the microwave for about 20 to 60 seconds.

# Sourdough Starter Recipe 3

## 100% Hydration Sourdough Starter

### Ingredients

50 grams or 4 tablespoons water, for 6 days

50 grams or 6 tablespoons whole grain flour, for 6 days

### *Equipment*

1 pint mason jar or other glass container

Rag from an old, clean cotton

### Directions

1. First, add 50 grams of whole grain or organic flour and 50 grams of water in a glass jar and then stir well to mix. Scrap off any bits from the edges down to the bottom.

2. Cover the glass jar with piece of old, clean cotton or other breathable material and then screw it on with the ring that comes with the mason jar.

3. Place the mixture at room temperature or about 70 to 75 degrees F and let it sit for approximately 24 hours.

4. On the second day, add another 50 grams of water and 50 grams of whole grain or organic flour. Stir the mixture well and scrap down the sides. Cover and set the mixture at room temperature for another 24 hours.

5. In day 3, add 50 grams each flour and water. Stir the sourdough starter and scrap down the side. Cover the mixture and set it aside for another 24 hours. You might be seeing some bubbles 1 hour after feeding, which is a good sign.

6. In day 4, discard the sourdough starter mixture while reserving only 25 grams. In a clean jar add 25 grams of the sourdough starter mixture and then add 50 grams of water and 50 grams of flour.

7. Stir the sourdough starter mixture well. Scrap down the sides and seal the jar. Set the mixture for another 24 hours.

8. In day 5, add an additional 50 grams of water and 50 grams of flour and stir well. Cover the contents and set aside for another day.

9. Come day 6, add in 50 grams of water and 50 grams of flour and stir to mix. Scrape down any bits down the sides and cover the sourdough starter for another 24 hours or so.

10. Continue with this method of feeding and discarding until your sourdough starter develops lots of bubbles and grows just after a few hours of feeding. This may take 5 to 14 days.

11. The sourdough starter is ready for use after feeding not only produces lots of bubbles but also doubles in size.

12. To speed up the time it takes for the sourdough starter to be ready for use, feed it every 12 hours instead and use flour made of whole grains as these have a higher amount of natural yeast.

13. You can also consider letting the sourdough starter rest in the shade during afternoons. Fresh air can facilitate the wild yeast.

14. In case your house is colder than the recommended temperature, look for a warm setting like the top of appliances that produce heat such as the fridge or on a heating pad. Also feed the starter with warm water or wrap it with a warm towel.

## Sourdough Naan

## Yields: 8 Pieces

## Ingredients

5 tablespoons melted butter

1 pinch of kosher salt

1 teaspoon baking powder

2 cups all purpose flour

1/4 cup thick plain Greek yogurt

1/2 cup warm milk

1 cup 100% hydration starter discard, unfed

## Directions

1. Combine the already made sourdough starter, yogurt and milk in a large bowl until smooth.

2. Add in the all-purpose flour, salt and baking powder and stir the ingredients to incorporate until you get tacky dough.

3. Cover the dough using a damp cloth and allow it to rise in a warm place for approximately 2 to 3 hours.

4. To test if ready, carefully dent the dough using your knuckle and see if it springs back. If it springs back, it is ready.

5. Dump the dough on thinly floured surface and knead until smooth or for 1 to 2 minutes. don't add a lot of flour as long as the dough isn't sticky.

6. Over medium-high heat, heat a heavy cast iron. Cut the dough into 8 pieces and roll individual pieces to approximately 1/4 inch thickness.

7. Add a little amount of flour on your work surface as well as on the rolling pin to help you roll the dough pieces.

8. Brush one side of the dough roll with melted butter and put it on the hot skillet the buttered side facing down.

9. Cook the naan until the dough begins to bubble and release from the skillet, or for approximately 1 minute.

10. Brush the other side with butter, flip the naan and cook for another 1 minute or so.

11. Transfer the naan to a plate and keep it covered with a kitchen towel to keep warm.

12. Repeat the procedure with the other rolls of dough and then serve.

13. You can also keep the naan refrigerated in an airtight container for not more than 3 days. Then you can just reheat the naan on a hot skillet a few minutes on both sides.

# Chocolate Sourdough Cake

## Yields 3 9" cake rounds

## Ingredients

*For Cake*

2 large eggs

3/4 cup dark cocoa powder, unsweetened

1 1/2 teaspoons baking soda

1 teaspoon salt

2 teaspoons vanilla extract

1 cup butter, melted and cooled

1 1/2 cups sugar

2 cups flour

1 cup milk

1 cup "fed" sourdough starter

Optional: 1 teaspoon espresso powder

*Cream Cheese Frosting*

6 cups powdered sugar

1/2 teaspoon salt

1 tablespoon vanilla extract

2 sticks unsalted butter

3 (8oz) bricks cream cheese

**Directions**

1. To make the cake batter, mix the all-purpose flour, milk and the sourdough starter.

2. Cover and allow the mixture to sit for about 2 to 3 hours so as to expand a little bit.

3. Preheat your oven to 350 degrees F. Meanwhile trace 3 cake pan circles onto a parchment paper and set aside.

4. Using some butter, grease 3 9-inch round cake pans and place a parchment paper circle in the bottom. Grease the circles and tap a layer of flour in.

5. In a separate bowl, beat together butter, espresso powder, cocoa, baking soda, salt, vanilla and sugar until you get a grainy mixture.

6. Add in the eggs, individually, and beat after each addition. Slowly mix the egg and chocolate with the sourdough starter flour mixture and stir until you get a smooth consistency.

7. Divide the batter evenly among 3 cake pans and bake for approximately 20 minutes making sure that you rotate the cake halfway through.

8. Remove the cake from the oven and let it cool on a wire rack for about 10 minutes. Set the cakes on the wire rack to cool fully.

9. To prepare the cream cheese frosting, first cream together the cream cheese and butter until you get a smooth consistency.

10. Add in salt and vanilla extract, and mix well. Add in the powdered sugar slowly until all the sugar has been incorporated.

11. In case you find the frosting too thick, add 1 to 2 teaspoons of water or instead add some more sugar in case it's too thin.

## Peanut Butter Cookies

### Yields 1 dozen

### Ingredients

1/3 cup granulated sugar, for rolling cookies

1/4 teaspoon salt

1 egg

1 teaspoon vanilla

1/2 teaspoon baking soda

1/2 teaspoon baking powder

1 cup flour or more

1/2 cup brown sugar

1/2 cup butter

1/2 cup peanut butter

1/2 cup 100% hydration starter discard

### Directions

# Starter Sourdough

1. Preheat your oven to 350 degrees F. Meanwhile, get a silicon-baking mat or a parchment paper and line 2 baking sheets; set aside.

2. Whisk together eggs, brown sugar, butter, peanut butter, vanilla extract and the sourdough starter in a large bowl until well blended.

3. In a separate medium bowl, whisk together the all-purpose flour, baking soda, baking powder and salt.

4. Pour the dry mixture into the wet ingredients mixture and stir to mix. The dough should appear soft and not sticky; otherwise you can add a little more flour until you can easily form a ball.

5. Get a cookie scoop and roll the dough into various balls and then roll the balls in the brown sugar.

6. Put the cookie balls onto the baking sheets and press them down using a fork to make criss-cross lines.

7. Bake the cookies until golden brown and soft, or for approximately 10 to 12 minutes.

8. Let the cookies cool while on the cookie sheet for around 1 to 2 minutes. Transfer from the wire rack to fully cool down. Serve and enjoy!

9. You can store the cookies on the counter in an airtight container for up to 4 days. Alternatively, let the cookies cool fully then put them in a freezer bag and keep frozen for not more than 2 months.

10. To get flatter, crispier cookies and with strong sourdough flavor, you should use an aged or sour unfed sourdough starter. Alternatively use a newer fed sourdough starter for softer and "normal" flavor peanut butter cookies.

## Chocolate Brownies

**Serves 9**

**Ingredients**

1/4 cup cocoa powder

1/2 cup 100% hydration starter discard

2 whole eggs

1 teaspoon vanilla extract

1 teaspoon salt

1/2 cup sugar

1/2 cup unsalted butter, cut into 1 stick

3/4 cup chopped bittersweet chocolate

**Directions**

1. Preheat your oven to 325 degrees F.

2. Line a metal square baking pan measuring 9 by 9 inch with parchment paper and coat with butter. Do not leave the paper hanging over the edges.

3. Melt butter and chocolate in the microwave, a saucepan or double boiler while stirring the mixture often so as not to boil.

4. Pour the butter and melted chocolate into a big bowl and whisk in vanilla extract, salt and sugar.

5. Add in the eggs, individually, as you whisk after each addition. Sift the cocoa powder over the melted butter and chocolate and stir until incorporated.

6. Add in the sourdough starter and stir until mixed, and then transfer the batter into a well-prepared baking pan.

7. Bake until if you insert a toothpick it comes out clean, or for approximately 30 to 40 minutes.

8. Cool the pan for another 20 minutes and gently lift the parchment paper out.

9. Let the brownies cool fully on a wire rack and cut them into squares.

10. To get cake-like sourdough starter brownies, try using full amount of sourdough starter discard or instead use 1/4 cup of sourdough starter for denser and chewer brownies.

# Cranberry Biscuits

**Serves 12**

**Ingredients**

*For Blondies*

1/2 cup dried cranberries

1/2 teaspoon salt

1/2 teaspoon baking powder

3/4 cup flour

2 teaspoons vanilla

1 egg

1 cup sourdough starter

3/4 cup brown sugar

1/3 cup butter, melted and cooled

*For Cream Cheese Frosting*

1/2 cup dried cranberries

6 ounces white chocolate chips

1 tablespoon orange zest

2 tablespoons milk

1 cup powdered sugar

1 package cream cheese

## Directions

1. To make the blondies, preheat your oven to 350 degrees F.

2. Mix the all-purpose flour, salt and baking powder in a medium bowl.

3. In a separate big bowl, whisk together brown sugar and melted butter and then whisk in the sourdough starter until it is fully incorporated.

4. Whisk in vanilla extract and eggs, and then fold in the dry ingredients mixture.

5. Add in the cranberries and pour the batter into a greased 8 by 8 inch pan. Bake for approximately 30 minutes.

6. Cool fully and then start preparing the cream cheese frosting.

7. In a bowl, whip together milk, powdered sugar, lemon zest and cream cheese until incorporated.

8. Pour this frosting over the cool bars and smooth. Spread some dried cranberries on top.

9. Melt the almond bark or chocolate chips and drizzle on top.

10. Finally cut the bar with the chocolate still soft and enjoy!

## Sourdough Crepes

**Serves 10**

### Ingredients

1 tablespoons sugar

2 tablespoons melted butter + 6 tablespoons more

1 pinch of sea salt

1/4 cup whole milk

1 cup sourdough starter

2 eggs

Preferred toppings

### Directions

1. Combine all the ingredients in the blender until smooth and blended.

2. Add in a sufficient amount of milk to make a thin batter of whipping cream or double cream consistency.

3. Allow the thin batter to rest for a minimum of 30 minutes in the fridge.

4. Over medium heat, preheat a frying pan and then once hot add a teaspoon of butter.

5. Allow the butter to melt and then add 1/4 cup of batter, as you tilt and swirl the pan so that it reaches the edges and coats the entire bottom of the pan.

6. Cook the batter until set and the bottom has light brown spots, or for a minute or so.

7. Use a spatula to flip the crepe and cook until they are almost crispy or for another 30 seconds or so.

8. You can then slide out of the pan and serve alongside your preferred filling or instead keep it frozen until ready to serve.

## Sourdough Popovers

**Serves 6**

**Ingredients**

1 teaspoon nutmeg, freshly grated

1 teaspoon black pepper

1 tablespoon kosher salt

2 tablespoons fresh parsley, finely chopped

1 cup flour

3/4 teaspoon salt

1/2 cup starter

3 large eggs

1 cup milk

**Directions**

1. Preheat your oven to 450 degrees F. Place a muffin tin in the oven as you preheat.

2. Warm milk in a small saucepan until it is warm to touch. Mix the warm milk with the sourdough starter, salt and eggs.

3. Add in nutmeg, pepper, parsley and the flour. Mix until well incorporate but you still have a few lumps.

4. Gently remove the muffin tin from the oven and coat it with nonstick spray. Pour the batter into the muffin pan.

5. If you are using an ordinary muffin pan, just fill the wells entirely and space the popovers around to have empty cups in between the full ones. In case you're using an actual popover pan, just fill it to almost the top.

6. Bake for approximately 15 minutes and then lower the temperature to 375 degrees F.

7. Bake until golden brown, or for another 15 to 20 minutes.

8. Remove from the oven and serve while hot!

## Sourdough Cornbread

**Serves 8**

**Ingredients**

1/2 teaspoon baking soda

2 teaspoon baking powder

1 teaspoon sea salt

1/2 cup melted butter

2 eggs

1/4 cup maple syrup

1 cup unbleached flour

1 cup cornmeal

1 cup milk

1 cup sourdough starter

**Directions**

1. Mix the unbleached flour, cornmeal, milk and the sourdough starter and cover the mixture.

2. Let the contents rest on the counter for about 8 to 24 hours. Meanwhile preheat your oven to 350 degrees F.

3. Whisk together melted butter, eggs, maple syrup and sea salt in a small bowl and stir the wet ingredients into the soured batter.

4. Sprinkle the mixture with baking soda and baking powder and stir until blended.

5. Transfer the batter into a greased 8 inch cast iron skillet or two 5 by 9 inch bread pan or 12 muffin pans.

6. Bake the batter for 15 minutes for muffins or for 35 minutes for bread. Insert a toothpick at the center of the bread to test for readiness.

7. Remove the bread from the oven and let it cool down. Slice and enjoy!

## Oat Quick Bread

## Serves 12

## Ingredients

1 tablespoons caster sugar

1/2 teaspoon baking soda

Zest of 1 lemon

1/4 cup slivered almonds

1 cup oats

1/2 teaspoon almond extract

1/2 cup milk

1/2 cup 100% hydration starter

1 egg

1/2 cup brown sugar

1/2 cup butter, melted and cooled

1/2 cup + 1 tablespoon flour

4 plums

# Starter Sourdough

## Directions

1. Preheat your oven to 350 degrees F and then slice a plum into thin slices. Set it aside.

2. Dice the rest of the plums and toss with a tablespoon of flour. Set the mixture aside.

3. Mix the sourdough starter with melted butter, milk, lemon zest, almond extract, eggs and brown sugar.

4. Add in 1/4 cup flour and the baking powder and mix well. Slowly fold in the floured plums.

5. Transfer the batter into a greased 9 by 11 loaf and smooth it on the top.

6. Layer a few plum slices and sprinkle a tablespoon of caster sugar on the batter.

7. Bake until if you insert a toothpick at the middle it comes out clean, or for 45 to 55 minutes.

8. Let the pan cool for approximately 10 minutes and then turn the bread onto a wire rack to cool fully. Serve!

## Sourdough Granola Bars

**Serves 9 bars**

**Ingredients**

1 cup sourdough starter

2/3 cup chocolate chips

1/3 cup maple syrup

2 tablespoons wheat germ

2 tablespoons flax seeds

1 1/2 cups oats

1/3 cup pepitas

1/3 cup chopped walnuts

1 cup dried fruit

1/3 cup uncooked quinoa

**Directions**

1. Preheat your oven to 350 degrees F.

2. Meanwhile in a large bowl combine all the ingredients and then press the mixture into an 8 by 8 inch baking pan.

3. Bake until the granola are golden, or for 20 to 25 minutes.

4. Let the granola cool fully then cut them into bars and enjoy.

## Hot Dog Buns

### Yields 9 buns

### Ingredients

170g 100% sourdough starter

27g softened butter

37g honey

10g salt

300g water

233g all purpose flour

200g whole wheat flour

*Topping*

Egg white

Sesame seeds

### Directions

1. Mix all the ingredients apart from 30 grams water in the bowl of a stand mixer that has a dough hook attachment.

2. Mix the dough on low speed for approximately 4 minutes, or until blended together. In case the batter is not medium soft, add in a little water in each addition.

3. Continue to mix at medium speed until the gluten is developed. Add the reserved water and continue to mix until all the water has blended in. You should get soft dough.

4. Ferment the dough in a well-sealed bowl for 2 hours 30 minutes at room temperature. You should fold the dough at 50 minutes and 100 minutes of fermenting.

5. Cut the dough into 9 pieces each weighing about 100 grams and shape the pieces into a hot dog bun.

6. Put the buns on a baking sheet lined with parchment paper.

7. Cover the dough with a tea towel and let it rest for about 3 hours or so.

8. Preheat your oven to 400 degrees F, and prepare steam for baking too.

9. Whisk together a teaspoon of water and egg white in a small bowl and brush the buns with this mixture.

10. Sprinkle with a little sesame seeds and bake with steam for approximately 8 minutes, and then without steam until the buns are well browned, or for 20 to 25 minutes.

11. Cool the buns on a wire rack, and then slice and enjoy!

# Sourdough Donuts

**Serves 12**

**Ingredients**

Oil for frying

1/3 cup buttermilk

1/2 teaspoon salt

1/4 teaspoon cinnamon

1/2 cup sugar

2 cups flour

1 egg

1/2 teaspoon baking soda

1 teaspoon baking powder

2 tablespoons oil

1/2 cup sourdough starter

**Directions**

1. Preheat a frying pan with sufficient oil to fry in, and then let it get to 360 degrees F.

2. Line a plate with some paper towels and set the plate aside.

3. Mix the all-purpose flour, baking soda, cinnamon, sugar, baking powder and salt in a medium bowl.

4. Mix together sourdough starter, milk, eggs and the oil in a large bowl.

5. Mix together the sourdough starter milk mixture with the flour mixture until fully incorporated.

6. Sprinkle a little flour on the counter surface and dump the dough from the bowl. Knead the dough until it comes together, or for 3 to 4 times.

7. Sprinkle the dough with some flour and roll it into 2-inch thick log.

8. Cut the dough into donuts.

9. Fry the donuts for 1 to 2 minutes on every side.

10. You can then drain the donuts on paper towel and coat them with sugar, cinnamon and powdered sugar, or glazed. Serve!

## Sourdough Pasta

**Serves 6**

**Ingredients**

2 eggs

1.5 cups flour

1/2 cup sourdough starter

**Directions**

1. Transfer the sourdough starter into a mixing bowl and add in egg, and flour. Mix until you get a ball of flour.

2. Let the dough sit on your counter for a few hours, preferably overnight in case it takes longer to rise.

3. Transfer the flour ball onto a well-floured surface and roll it as thin as you can.

4. Slice the noodles into preferred shapes and add any filling you want. You can boil the sourdough pasta or let it dry out until ready to serve.

## Sourdough Pancakes

**Serves 12**

**Ingredients**

2 tablespoons vegetable oil

2 tablespoons brown sugar

1 teaspoon salt

1 teaspoon baking soda

2/3 cup milk

1 egg

2.5 cups flour

1.5 cups warm water

1 cup sourdough starter

**Directions**

1. The night before, begin by combining the flour, warm water and the sourdough starter in a plastic or glass bowl.

2. Lightly cover the mixture using a saran wrap and let it sit preferably overnight.

3. The following morning, mix together vegetable oil, sugar, salt, baking soda, milk and the egg in a medium bowl until well incorporated.

4. Whisk the vegetable oil and egg mixture into the sourdough starter mixture and let the contents stand undisturbed for about 5 minutes or so.

5. Pour ¼ cupful batter onto a hot griddle and cook until the bottom is golden and the bubbles have formed on top of the pancakes.

6. Flip the pancake and cook the other side until golden and serve.

# Pizza Crescent Rolls

## Serves 12

## Ingredients

2 cups shredded mozzarella cheese

2 cups Pepperoni slices

2/3 cup fed and active sourdough starter discard

4 tablespoons butter

1 tablespoon sugar

1/2 teaspoon baking soda

1/2 teaspoon salt

1 teaspoon baking powder

1 cup flour

## Directions

1. Begin by preheating your oven to 400 degrees F.

2. Whisk together all-purpose flour, sugar, baking soda, baking powder and salt.

3. Rub or cut in the butter until its course, and then mix in the starter. Stir the ingredients together until you have soft dough.

4. Carefully knead the dough for approximately 1 minute and then cut the dough into two.

5. Roll each dough half on a well floured surface to form a 9 inch circle. Cut individual circle into about 6 wedges or so.

6. Put shredded cheese and the pepperonis slices on each of the 12 wedges and then roll up the ingredients beginning from the big bottom up to the small point.

7. Put the crescent rolls in a baking sheet, and bake them for approximately 12 minutes. Serve!

8. In case you want to get less fluffy crescent rolls, you can try using unfed sourdough starter discard instead.

# Conclusion

We have come to the end of the book. Thank you for reading and congratulations on reading until the end.

I hope you are excited to try out the various recipes for starter sourdough and make delicious pastries with it. All the best as you experiment.

If you found the book valuable, can you recommend it to others? One way to do that is to post a review on Amazon.

Please leave a review for this book on Amazon by visiting the page below:

https://amzn.to/2VMR5qr

Thank you, and good luck!

Printed in Great Britain
by Amazon